T0036697

Who Was
John Lewis?

by Crystal Hubbard

illustrated by Stephen Marchesi

Penguin Workshop

For Robin Washington,
whose work inspired mine—CH

For my friends at old A & D—SM

PENGUIN WORKSHOP
An imprint of Penguin Random House LLC, New York

First published in the United States of America by Penguin Workshop,
an imprint of Penguin Random House LLC, New York, 2023

Visit us online at penguinrandomhouse.com.

Library of Congress Control Number: 2023023630

Printed in the United States of America

ISBN 9780593658512 (paperback)   10 9 8 7 6 5 4 3 2 1 WOR
ISBN 9780593658529 (library binding)   10 9 8 7 6 5 4 3 2 1 WOR

Contents

Who Was John Lewis? 1

An Early Calling 4

A Young Man with a Mission 16

The Cost of Freedom 30

The Power of Peaceful Protests 44

Plunging into Politics 54

A Mission Guided by Martin 65

The Activist Turned Author 84

The End of a Life of Good Trouble 91

Timelines 104

Bibliography 106

Who Was John Lewis?

John Lewis, the twenty-five-year-old chairman of the Student Nonviolent Coordinating Committee (SNCC) linked arms with the people standing at his sides. With hundreds of people behind him, he steadily walked across the Edmund Pettus Bridge. He and the people with him were walking from Selma, Alabama, to the state's capital, Montgomery. The long walk, he hoped, would make lawmakers take notice of the fact that there was a very big problem.

Black people were having a difficult, if not impossible, time registering to vote and casting their votes if they did manage to register.

They were bullied and beaten. They were threatened with being fired from their jobs. Their homes were vandalized, all because they wanted to use the one thing they could to change the way they had to live: They wanted to vote.

If he was afraid, John and the people with him did not show it, even though they saw police on foot and on horseback, and ordinary people with weapons, waiting at the end of the bridge. Moving ever closer to the angry line of people blocking the end of the bridge, John hoped for the best. After swallowing over the hard, dry lump in his throat, John took a deep breath, and began to sing a hymn he knew from church.

The other marchers sang with him, and they kept marching and singing even after a loud, furious voice coming through a megaphone ordered them to go back where they came from. Armed only with songs and hope, John and the marchers from Selma continued the path they had started on that day, March 7, 1965, which would become known as Bloody Sunday.

Bloody Sunday

CHAPTER 1
An Early Calling

Willie Mae and Eddie Lewis

On February 21, 1940, John Robert Lewis was born just outside the town of Troy, Alabama. His parents, Willie Mae and Eddie Lewis, were sharecroppers, people who farm land that belongs to someone else. They had to pay the landowner money and also a share of the crops they raised on the land. Sharecroppers often earned very little, no matter how hard they worked.

It took many years, but Willie Mae and Eddie earned enough money to buy a 110-acre farm of their own, where they grew cotton, peanuts, and corn. Eddie built a small farmhouse for Willie Mae and their ten children. The house did not have electricity or running water. The toilet was in a separate little building outside the house.

John's parents were proud of their house and farm. They taught John that it was important for people to have something of their very own.

John was the third of Willie Mae and Eddie's ten children. John's six brothers were named Adolph, Sammy, William, Grant, Edward, and Freddie. His three sisters were named Ethel, Rosa, and Ora.

John's older siblings worked on the farm every day. When they were not working on the farm, Eddie drove a school bus and Willie Mae worked as a maid to bring in more money. By the time he was five years old, John knew he did not want to be a farmer or a bus driver when he grew up. John wanted to be a preacher.

On the farm, John's job was to feed the chickens and collect their eggs. He loved the chickens, especially the soft and fluffy young chicks.

Other people thought chickens were dirty and smelled bad. John knew how smart the chickens were. He named them and told them the Bible stories he learned in church. He even preached to them! John cared for the chickens so much, he protested when his parents wanted to cook chicken for dinner.

John was a good student who loved school. His parents encouraged John to get an education, but there was so much work to do on the farm, especially when it was time to harvest crops. His parents wanted him to stay home from school in order to help. But John did not want to miss any school days during the harvest season. He would

sneak away from the farm and run to catch the bus to school.

Because many schools for Black students were underfunded, John's school did not have many books. There were even fewer books at home. And John loved reading. When he tried to visit the public library in Troy to get more books, John learned that the Troy Public Library was segregated. (*Segregation* means forced separation, as in separate areas and services for Black and white people.) Unfortunately, the Troy library was for white people only.

In 1951, when he was eleven years old, John's uncle took him to visit Buffalo, New York. John saw big differences between schools and life for Black people in the North. People in the North might not have always been friendly, but John could go into the same stores as white people. He could also sit anywhere he wanted on buses.

Jim Crow Laws

Segregation in the United States was promoted through Jim Crow laws from the 1880s to the 1960s. The name Jim Crow came from a character in minstrel shows, who was always played by a white actor whose face was covered in black makeup.

The most well-known Jim Crow laws banned marriage between people of different races and insisted that businesses, libraries, hospitals, restaurants, and other public places keep Black and white people separated.

States from Delaware to California, from North Dakota to Texas, and states and cities in between were even allowed to legally punish people who befriended people of another race.

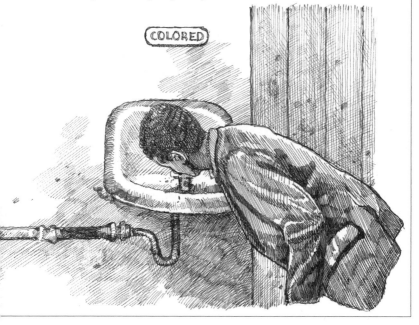

COLORED

In southern states, like Alabama, Black and white people were kept separated. Jim Crow laws were enforced to keep people of different races apart.

In the southern part of the United States, Black people and white people did not live in the same neighborhoods. Black people had to ride in the back of buses. They had separate schools from white people. The schools for Black children were not as well equipped or as nice as schools for white children, even though they were supposed to be equal.

John hated Jim Crow laws because he knew how wrong they were.

CHAPTER 2
A Young Man with a Mission

In 1954, the Supreme Court of the United States decided that "separate but equal" schools for Black and white children was wrong. The legal case was called *Brown v. Board of Education*. The Supreme Court's decision was supposed to make schools better for Black children. John was disappointed when nothing changed in Alabama.

One night in 1955, something gave fifteen-year-old John hope. He listened to a preacher on the radio. His name was Martin Luther King Jr., and he spoke about putting an end to the unfair treatment Black people had suffered for so long. John was very interested in Martin's work that led to the Montgomery Bus Boycott. The boycott began on December 5, 1955, four days after a Black woman named Rosa Parks refused to give up her seat on a bus to a white man. The boycott was organized as a way to force the end of segregation on buses. John followed the news of the boycott from its beginning to its end on December 20, 1956.

Martin Luther King Jr.

Rosa Parks (1913–2005)

Rosa Louise McCauley Parks is known as "the first lady of civil rights" and "mother of the freedom movement" because she refused to give up her seat on a bus to a white man in Montgomery, Alabama, on December 1, 1955.

Rosa was born on February 4, 1913, in Tuskegee, Alabama. She was raised on her mother's parents' farm. Rosa married Raymond Parks in 1932. He was involved with the NAACP, the National Association for the Advancement of Colored People. Rosa joined the NAACP and became active in the civil rights movement in 1943.

She was working as a seamstress when the NAACP chose her to be part of a planned effort to protest Jim Crow laws that forced Black people to sit in the back of buses. Rosa was arrested when she refused to give up her seat on the bus for a white passenger and spent a night in jail. But her peaceful protest inspired Black people to quit riding the buses and is thought to be the start of the civil rights movement.

Martin Luther King Jr.'s speeches about making change by nonviolent methods inspired John. He decided that he wanted to do something to help end the injustice toward Black people.

When John graduated from the Pike County Training High School in 1957, he wanted to attend Troy State College, an all-white college in his hometown. His application was rejected because he was Black.

Troy State College

John was so upset, he wrote to Martin for advice. The famous pastor was so impressed, he invited John to Montgomery, the capital of Alabama. Martin also sent John a Greyhound bus ticket for the fifty-mile trip. Montgomery was Martin's hometown and the place where he began his fight for civil rights for Black people.

Martin and John, who he called "the boy from Troy," met in March 1958 at the First Baptist Church. Martin told John that they could get the money to pay for a legal battle to attend Troy State College, but it would not be easy. White people violently fought against desegregation. They didn't want to see an end to separating people by skin color. It took only one person to desegregate an entire university, and John wanted to be that person. Martin warned John that he or his family could be hurt if John tried to desegregate Troy State College.

John's parents convinced him to attend American Baptist Theological Seminary in Nashville, Tennessee, instead. There, John would learn to be a preacher. Willie Mae and Eddie had little money to pay for college, so John worked when he was not studying or in class. Willie Mae advised her son to work hard, study hard, and to stay out of trouble. John graduated from the seminary, but while he was there he did go ahead with his application to all-white Troy State University in his hometown.

American Baptist Theological Seminary

Martin Luther King Jr. (1929–1968)

Martin Luther King Jr. was born in Atlanta, Georgia. His father, Martin Luther King Sr., was a civil rights activist who taught Martin Jr. the importance of peaceful protesting and nonviolent confrontation. Martin Jr. was a very good student who skipped the ninth grade and part of eleventh grade, winning a speech contest before graduating at age fifteen. His way with words was one of Martin Jr.'s greatest assets in the fight for civil rights.

Martin grew up to be a Baptist minister who was recognized as the leader of the civil rights movement in America in 1955 with the success of the Montgomery Bus Boycott. (The boycott was a reaction to the arrest of Rosa Parks.) He became America's most outspoken champion of civil rights after delivering his famous "I Have a

Dream" speech on the steps of the Lincoln Memorial during the 1963 March on Washington for Jobs and Freedom.

John itched to be a part of Martin's movement for civil rights. He paid close attention in workshops that taught action through nonviolence. The idea of fighting for something in a peaceful way interested John very much. He took part in peaceful activities to bring about change. Sit-ins (a protest where demonstrators sit down and refuse to leave) were one kind of those activities.

In 1960, John helped create the Student Nonviolent Coordinating Committee, or SNCC. The first time John was arrested was on February 27, 1960. He was twenty years old. He and other SNCC members sat down at a whites-only lunch counter at a Woolworth's store in Nashville, Tennessee. The students took seats in a polite, orderly manner. Angry white customers threw food at John and his companions and poured beverages over their heads. They spit at them and called them horrible names.

They tried to yank the students off their seats. The students kept sitting up straight. They did not speak to one another or the people attacking them. They did not fight back, not even when the police arrived and arrested them instead of the violent people attacking them.

"I didn't necessarily want to go to jail," John said in a 1973 interview for the Southern Oral History Program. "But we knew . . . it would help solidify the student community and the Black community as a whole. The student community

did rally. The people heard that we had been arrested and before the end of the day, five hundred students made it into the downtown area to occupy other stores and restaurants. At the end of the day, ninety-eight of us were in jail."

The sit-ins worked. Nashville desegregated its lunch counters on May 10, 1960.

CHAPTER 3
The Cost of Freedom

President Dwight D. Eisenhower

In 1960, President Dwight D. Eisenhower signed the Civil Rights Act of 1960 into law after the US Supreme Court ruled that segregation on buses and trains was illegal. Separate water fountains, bathrooms, seating in theaters, and other forms of segregation were also against the law. The United States government did little to enforce the ruling against segregation. Men, women, and students like John challenged segregation by taking Freedom Rides.

Freedom Riders were groups of Black and white people who rode buses through Alabama, Mississippi, and Louisiana to protest segregation. John was one of the first Freedom Riders. John, now twenty-one, had recently graduated from the seminary with a degree in religion. In May 1961, he was one of thirteen men and women who boarded a bus in Washington, DC, headed to New Orleans, Louisiana.

Freedom Riders

Soon after the trip began, the Freedom Ride stopped in Rock Hill, South Carolina. John was attacked for riding on the bus with white people, but he made it back onto the bus. In Montgomery, Alabama, a white mob beat John so badly, they knocked him out. John did not let violence stop him. He continued to ride for freedom. In Jackson, Mississippi, John went into a restroom that was labeled for white people. Charged with disorderly conduct for using a restroom illegally reserved for white people only, John was arrested on May 24, 1961. He spent thirty-seven days in a prison called Parchman Farm.

Parchman Prison

"During the time I was being beaten and other times when I was being beaten, I had what I called an executive session with myself. I said I'm gonna take it, I'm prepared. On the Freedom Ride, I was prepared to die," John said.

John enrolled in Fisk University in 1961 to study religion and philosophy. Two years later, in 1963, he became head of the SNCC. It was an unpaid position with a lot of work, but

President John F. Kennedy

John was glad to be in charge. He became known as one of the "Big Six," a group of Black leaders who met with President John F. Kennedy to discuss ways to protect rights for Black people.

John was also one of the speakers at the March on Washington for Jobs and Freedom. The event on August 28, 1963, is more well-known for Martin's famous "I Have a Dream" speech. But John spoke just before Martin that day. The twenty-three-year-old sounded like a preacher as he stood on the steps of the Lincoln Memorial and spoke with confidence. "We are tired. We are tired of being beaten by policemen. We are tired of seeing our people locked up in jail over and over again . . . We want our freedom and we want it now. We do not want to go to jail. But we will go to jail if this is the price we must pay for love, brotherhood, and true peace."

Fisk University

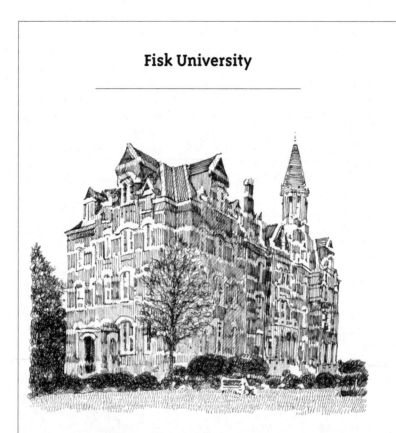

John Ogden, Reverend Erastus Milo Cravath, and Reverend Edward P. Smith established the Fisk School in Nashville, Tennessee, six months after the end of the Civil War. They named the new school after General Clinton B. Fisk, who donated buildings and other necessities to it.

Fisk's first classes were held on January 9, 1866. The first students shared a common history of slavery and poverty and ranged in age from seven to seventy. They also shared the desire to learn. The school was legally made a university on August 22, 1867.

The Big Six

The Big Six was the name given to the most prominent leaders of the civil rights movement of the 1960s. They were six men from different professions who came together to work for equality for Black people.

The "Big Six" civil rights leaders: John Lewis, Whitney Young Jr., A. Philip Randolph, Martin Luther King Jr., James Farmer Jr., and Roy Wilkins

John Lewis, who was still in college, was the youngest member of the group. Asa Philip Randolph was a labor organizer who helped Black workers on trains receive better pay and better working conditions. Dr. Martin Luther King Jr. was a minister and activist who won the Nobel Peace Prize in 1964 for his work toward civil rights. James Farmer Jr. created the Congress of Racial Equality, an organization dedicated to fighting for equality and racial harmony through nonviolence. Whitney Moore Young Jr. was a social worker dedicated to ending employment discrimination. Roy Wilkins began his career as a journalist, but he was most known for being the executive director of the National Association for the Advancement of Colored People (NAACP).

The march encouraged President Kennedy and Congress to write a new civil rights bill. The bill would make it illegal to treat people unfairly because of their skin color. President Kennedy

President Lyndon B. Johnson

was assassinated on November 22, 1963, before he could sign the bill into law. Lyndon B. Johnson became president, and he signed it. But southern states did not obey the Civil Rights Act of 1964. They continued to make life hard for Black people, especially when it came to voting.

In 1964, John and the SNCC planned voter registration drives during what was named the Mississippi Freedom Summer. Mississippi had the fewest Black voters, so John and other college students went out to help Black people register to vote and to teach them about its process. They also taught them the importance of voting. The SNCC also set up Freedom Schools for Black students that had better equipment and resources than the schools John had attended when he was younger.

Alabama, Mississippi, and other southern states made Black people take tests or pay a fee just to register to vote. Black people who registered to vote found their homes and jobs threatened. Threatening and harming people who want to register to vote or cast a vote is called voter suppression.

John took a journey far from Mississippi in September, when he and other civil rights

activists visited Africa. They began the trip in Guinea, where they spoke to young people about their experiences in the United States. John decided to visit Liberia, Ghana, Zambia, and Ethiopia. He met another rising civil rights figure, Malcolm X, in Nairobi, Kenya. John and Malcolm talked about the worldwide fight for Black civil rights and their hopes for the fight in America.

John arrives in Kenya

CHAPTER 4
The Power of Peaceful Protests

When John returned to the United States, he and other members of the SNCC teamed up with Martin's group, the Southern Christian Leadership Conference (SCLC), to do something

to help Black people register to vote. They decided on a peaceful march from Selma, Alabama, to the state capitol building in Montgomery. The shortest route by foot was fifty-four miles. They hoped to walk all day and all night, and if they managed it, the march would take three to five days. They hoped the march would bring attention to their cause.

Governor George Wallace

Alabama's governor, George Wallace, was in favor of segregation. And he did not want Black people to vote. He declared the march to Montgomery illegal, even though it was not. On March 7, 1965, John and Hosea Williams of the SCLC led hundreds of marchers, people from all different races and backgrounds, toward Montgomery. When they got to the Edmund Pettus Bridge in Selma, they linked arms. Two by two, singing hymns, they marched on the sidewalk. Even though the bridge had been closed to traffic, they stayed on the sidewalk to lawfully cross the bridge.

Governor Wallace called out the state police to stop the marchers. When the marchers got to the other side of the bridge, the police ordered them to turn around and go home. John and the other marchers stayed in place, arms linked, singing peacefully.

The state police, assisted by armed people who had quickly been made deputies (authorized to act as police, even though they were not trained), attacked the marchers with clubs, bullwhips, and tear gas. Some of the marchers were trampled by horses. Many of the marchers were injured and arrested. John's skull was fractured. Amelia Boynton, one of the local organizers of the march, was beaten to the ground.

Amelia Boynton

Newspapers all over the United States published photos of Amelia lying hurt. They printed photos of John being beaten by a state trooper. Television reports all over the world showed video footage of the peaceful marchers being brutalized by Alabama's state police and the citizens who were acting as deputies on their behalf.

Americans were outraged. The march to Montgomery was called Bloody Sunday because of the violence committed by the police and deputies. John spent two days in the hospital after Bloody Sunday. Two weeks later, he was again marching to Montgomery in support of voting rights for Black people.

The violence of the first march led President Johnson to get Congress to propose a new voting

rights bill to enable Black people to vote and register to vote without harassment or harm. In August 1965, President Johnson signed the bill and it became the Voting Rights Act.

President Johnson signs the Voting Rights Act

The Voting Rights Act of 1965

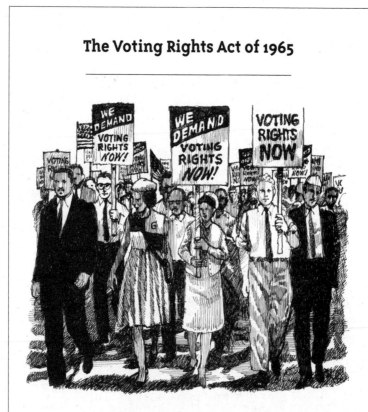

In the United States government, a bill summarizes what a potential law *should* do. Bills, which are suggestions for new laws, can be introduced by members of Congress. If the House of Representatives and the Senate vote to approve a bill, it gets sent to the president. If the president signs the bill, it becomes a law. Laws are also called Acts of Congress.

The Civil Rights Act of 1960, which struck down Jim Crow laws, was passed in order to reinforce the Civil Rights Act of 1957. The Voting Rights Act of 1965 was meant to outlaw voting discrimination against Black people in southern states where literacy tests, poll taxes, and other tactics were used to stop Black people from voting.

President Lyndon B. Johnson signed the Voting Rights Act on August 6, 1965. It was immediately effective. By the end of the year, a quarter of a million new Black voters were registered. The Voting Rights Act of 1965 was strengthened and readopted in 1970, 1975, and 1982 to withstand challenges from southern states still trying to suppress voting rights.

CHAPTER 5
Plunging into Politics

In 1966, John left the SNCC. He still believed in peaceful, nonviolent means to bring change. But he thought the group was taking a more aggressive direction. He worked for civil rights even as he continued his studies at Fisk. Since his first arrest in 1960, John had been arrested more than forty times at peaceful protests.

In 1967, he graduated from Fisk with a degree in religion and philosophy. He took a job in New York City as associate director of the Field Foundation, which worked to end poverty and inequality. John left the foundation for a chance to work in Atlanta, which was closer to Alabama and where Martin lived and worked.

He was hired to be the director of the Community Organization Project for the Southern Regional Council. John led Black and white people who worked to promote racial equality and prevent racial violence.

In Atlanta, John met a woman named Lillian Miles. She was very smart and worked as a librarian. She helped John get through April 4, 1968, one of the worst days of his life. It was the day his mentor and friend Martin was assassinated in Memphis, Tennessee.

John left the council for a little while so he could work on New York senator Robert F. Kennedy's campaign to become president of the United States. Robert was John F. Kennedy's brother. John Lewis was with Robert when, sadly, he was assassinated in Los Angeles on June 6, 1968.

John and Lillian got married six months later, on December 21, 1968. The next year, John was invited to Sweden to speak at a meeting of people from all over the world who were against the war going on in Vietnam. John asked a question that no one could answer: Why was President Johnson sending American troops thousands of miles away to fight a war in Vietnam while not sending troops to protect Black people fighting to uphold basic human rights in America?

President Johnson did eventually order troops to protect people peacefully protesting racial injustice.

Lillian was not overly interested in politics, but she was supportive of John's work as director of the Voter Education Project (VEP), a job he took in 1970. The VEP helped people register to vote and understand their voting and civil rights.

Under John's leadership, the VEP registered millions of Black people to vote. John believed that the right to vote was the most powerful tool an American, no matter their race, could have.

On March 3, 1975, John testified before a committee in Congress about the need to strengthen the Voting Rights Act. "Those who hold illegitimate power will not give it up voluntarily," Lewis said. He asked Congress to pass a permanent act to guarantee the protection

of Black voters all over the United States. John was awarded the Martin Luther King Jr. Nonviolent Peace Prize in 1975 for his continued work for civil rights.

Lillian and John

adopted a boy they named John-Miles in 1976. John and Lillian loved their young son very much.

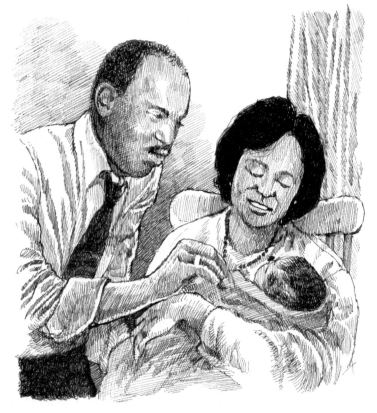

In 1977, President Jimmy Carter, a native of Georgia, asked John to lead ACTION, a national volunteer agency that oversaw groups

President Jimmy Carter

such as the Peace Corps. He accepted the position. But John wondered if he could be of more help to people if he worked in parts of the government that created and passed laws. He ran for election to Atlanta's city council in 1981, and he won.

In 1986, John ran for election to the US House of Representatives to represent Georgia's Fifth District. John, whose own parents had been prevented from voting, won the election. He officially became a United States representative. John was so good at representing the people of Georgia, he was reelected sixteen more times!

Being in Congress gave John more power as an activist. He could speak out for people whose voices were not being heard. He could help create laws that made America smarter and safer. After John was sworn into the US House of Representatives in 1987, he was put on two committees, then a third, and more. By 1995, John had worked his way up to serving on the Ways and Means Committee, which keeps track of how the United States government takes in and spends money.

John entered Congress with a very clear plan: He wanted to get laws passed that advanced civil rights, environmental issues, education, and health care. John's work as a representative showed his pursuit of Martin's desire to create a "beloved community," a nation committed to equality with a foundation of peace and justice for all.

CHAPTER 6
A Mission Guided by Martin

In 1995, John shared what guided his work in Congress. "I am a man who deeply believes in compassion and hope. A man who, day after day, struggles to build the bridges that will allow us all to come together in Dr. King's beloved community."

In 2001, John received the Profile in Courage Lifetime Achievement Award from the John F. Kennedy Library Foundation. This was the first

time the award for lifetime achievement had been given. John was chosen for the award because of his "extraordinary courage, leadership, vision and commitment to universal human rights."

When the Voting Rights Act was set to expire in 2007, John led the effort to refresh and renew the law. He objected to any amendments that would make it harder for people to vote. John knew the act needed to be preserved. "We cannot separate the debate today from our history and the past we have traveled." John knew that law was as necessary in 2006 as it had been in 1965.

John worked very hard to protect the gains of the civil rights movement and to celebrate and preserve its history. In his first term, he passed a bill that named a federal building in Atlanta after Dr. Martin Luther King Jr. Throughout his entire career, John proposed bills that would name other federal buildings after judges, lawyers,

Martin Luther King Jr. Federal Building

and activists who worked and even died to build the civil rights movement.

Every year, John returned to the Edmund Pettus Bridge in Selma, Alabama, to cross it once again. He invited all members of Congress to go with him. President Barack Obama, First Lady Michelle Obama, and their daughters, Malia and Sasha, joined John for the walk across the Edmund Pettus Bridge on March 2, 2015. This march commemorated the fiftieth anniversary of the Selma-to-Montgomery civil rights marches. Thousands of Americans walked right along with John and President Obama's family.

John had proposed legislation to build a national museum of African American history back in 1991. But it had taken many years to get enough support for his bill to build it. The bill to create the National Museum of African American History & Culture in Washington, DC, was signed into law in 2003 by President George W. Bush.

President George W. Bush

The museum's exhibits represent every era and area of African American history, from politics to sports to art. Permanent displays include items from the *São José Paquete D'África*, a slave ship that sank off the coast of South Africa in 1794, a drinking fountain labeled "Colored" from the Jim Crow era in the United States, and items from President Barack Obama's presidential campaign. One of the most striking displays in the museum is the coffin of Emmett Till, a fourteen-year-old boy who was tortured and lynched in 1955 for allegedly whistling at a white woman.

John publicly supported important human rights issues, including the rights of women, immigration rights, gun control, LGBTQ+ rights, and health care reform. John believed every American should be able to be treated by a doctor without going bankrupt. Fighting for health care reform reminded John of what it was like when he was younger and fighting for civil rights. He received angry letters and nasty phone calls from people who didn't agree with him. Angry protestors on the steps of the Capitol shouted furiously at him when he went to vote on a health care bill in 2010.

The National Museum
of African American History & Culture

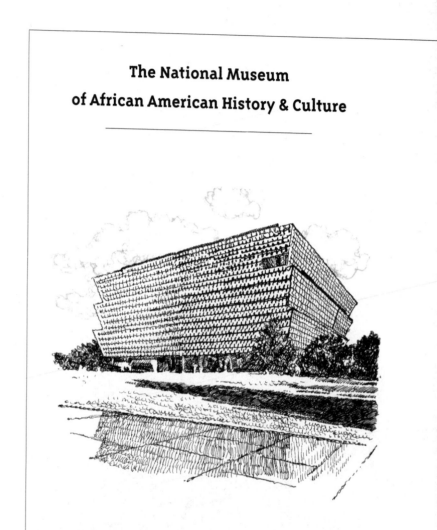

The National Museum of African American History & Culture opened in Washington, DC, on September 24, 2016, in a three-day celebration organized by producer Quincy Jones with a ceremony led by President Barack Obama.

The museum is the nineteenth part of the Smithsonian Institution, the largest museum complex in the world. The building's modern design represents African architecture and the ironwork of enslaved people from New Orleans. The ten-story museum houses more than 40,000 artifacts (with 3,500 on display). The museum had more than one million visitors in its first four months.

Emmett Till (1941–1955)

Emmett Till had been born and raised in Chicago, Illinois. While visiting relatives in Mississippi in 1955, fourteen-year-old Emmett encountered grocery clerk Carolyn Bryant who accused the young boy of whistling at her. In Mississippi in 1955, simply greeting a white person could mean trouble for a Black person. A few days after his encounter with Carolyn, her husband, Roy, and his half brother, J. W.

Milam, abducted Emmett. They beat him, tortured him, shot him, and threw his body in the Tallahatchie River. This kind of murder was called a lynching.

Mamie Till Bradley, Emmett's mother, insisted on having his coffin open during his funeral in Chicago. She wanted the world to see the brutality her son had suffered. In September 1955, Roy and J. W. were found innocent of Emmett's murder. In *Look* magazine in 1956, the two admitted that they were guilty of torturing and murdering Emmett. They were paid $4,000 for their story. In an interview in 2008, Carolyn Bryant admitted that she had lied about Emmett.

On March 29, 2022, President Joe Biden signed the Emmett Till Antilynching Act into law, which finally made lynching a federal hate crime. Upon her death in 2023, Carolyn had never been held accountable for the lie that led to Emmett's murder.

President Obama signs the Affordable Care Act

John was not scared off. He cast a vote for the Patient Protection and Affordable Care Act. The act would offer every American the chance to get health insurance they could afford. When the act passed, John said voting for it was one of the proudest moments of his career.

John was one of the congresspeople who proposed the Emmett Till Unsolved Civil Rights Crime Act in 2007. The act allowed authorities to open unsolved cases of suspected violence against Black people that were committed before 1970. President George W. Bush signed the act into law on October 7, 2008.

The first LBJ Liberty & Justice for All Award was given to John by the Lyndon Baines Johnson Foundation in 2010. The award is given to political leaders who do their jobs with civility and bipartisanship.

John Lewis with his LBJ Liberty & Justice for All Award

Civility is a fancy word for kindness and patience. Bipartisanship means working with people whose political party is different from yours. The late Supreme Court justice Ruth Bader Ginsburg and former president George H. W. Bush have also received this award.

In 2011, President Barack Obama awarded John the Presidential Medal of Freedom. The Medal of Freedom is the highest nonmilitary award that can be given to an American.

When President Obama was sworn into office as the forty-fourth president of the United States in 2008, John was onstage with him. He was the last living member of the civil rights activists who spoke on the steps of the Lincoln Memorial during the March on Washington in 1963. President Obama gave John a photograph commemorating the inauguration. Aware of how John's civil rights work helped lead to the election of America's first Black president, he signed the photo, "Because of you, John. Barack Obama."

In 2012, the one person with whom John most enjoyed sharing his work and good fortune passed away. His beloved wife Lillian died on December 31, 2012. John and Lillian had been married for forty-four years. John never remarried. He became even more dedicated to his work as a US representative. Never afraid of acting on what he thought was right, in 2019 John voted to impeach President Donald J. Trump after an investigation revealed that the president had abused his power and obstructed Congress in an investigation.

President Donald Trump

Barack Obama (1961–)

Barack Hussein Obama II was born in Honolulu, Hawaii, on August 4, 1961, to a white American mother and a Black Kenyan father. He spent part of his childhood in Indonesia. He was a very good student who attended the Punahou School in Hawaii on a scholarship from fifth to twelfth grade.

He graduated from Columbia University with a degree in political science in 1983. He completed a law degree from Harvard in 1991. He taught constitutional law at the University of Chicago Law School.

Elected to the US Senate in 2004, Barack served half of his six-year term before running for president of the United States. He defeated Republican Senator John McCain to become the forty-fourth president—and the first African American president—of the United States on November 4, 2008. He won more votes than any other presidential candidate up to that point and served as US president from 2009–2017.

A Black man named George Floyd was killed by police officers on May 25, 2020. John supported the protests against police violence and bias that broke out all over the United States after George Floyd's death. John visited Black Lives Matter Plaza in Washington, DC, in June.

The *Atlanta Journal-Constitution* stated Lewis was the "only former major civil rights leader who extended his fight for human rights and racial reconciliation to the halls of Congress . . . those who know him, from U. S. senators to 20-something congressional aides, called him 'the conscience of the U. S. Congress.' "

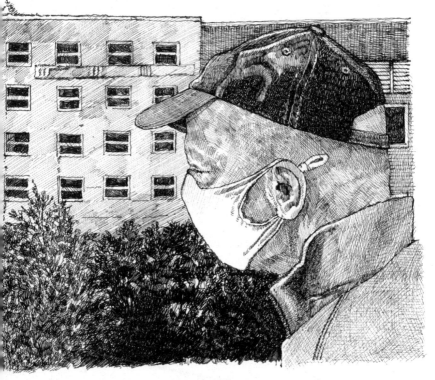

John in front of Black Lives Matter Plaza

CHAPTER 7
The Activist Turned Author

When John was a teenager, a comic book about  Martin Luther King Jr. sparked his interest in civil rights and equality. John wanted to inspire younger generations to pursue lives of service in the same way.

John cowrote a series of graphic novels with Andrew Aydin, hoping to reach a new generation of young activists. *March: Book One*, *Book Two*, and *Book Three* are detailed accounts of his life, from his early years to the pivotal events of his fight for civil rights. John's fourth graphic novel,

Run, is about the struggles that came after the passage of the Voting Rights Act of 1965. John's biography is titled *Walking with the Wind: A Memoir of the Movement.* Each of John's books were best sellers.

John's hard work writing the graphic novels was rewarded. In 2016, he and his coauthors,

Andrew Aydin and Nate Powell, won a National Book Award for Young People's Literature for *March: Book Three.*

John made history again by earning this award. This was the first time it was given to a comic or graphic novel. The award brought up a painful memory for John, and he came close to tears when he gave his speech to accept it.

"I remember in 1956, when I was sixteen years old, with some of my brothers and sisters and cousins, going down to the public library and trying to get library cards," John began, staring down at the award in his hands, with teary eyes. "We were told that libraries were for 'whites only' and not for 'coloreds.' To come here and receive

John, Andrew Aydin, and Nate Powell win the National Book Award

this award, this honor, is too much."

In 2017, *March: Book Three* also won the Coretta Scott King Author Award. The Coretta Scott King Award is named for Martin Luther King Jr.'s wife. It is awarded to African American authors of books for children and young adults. The book is an account of twenty-five-year-old John and the activists working with him to start a revolution of nonviolence as they worked for racial equality in the early 1960s. The book covers the time leading up to the march from Selma to Montgomery, Alabama. The March trilogy is named for that event.

John understood that reading was a key part of education. Schools throughout the United States gave John honorary degrees for his efforts to improve education over the years. Troy University, known as Troy State College when it rejected John's application because he was Black, issued

John an honorary doctor of laws degree in 1989. Between 1989 and 2019, John was awarded more than fifty honorary degrees! (An honorary degree is a degree earned through life and career experience rather than classroom study.)

John started to attend some of the annual comic book conventions, also known to fans as comic cons, to promote and sign his books. He went to one of the biggest, the San Diego Comic-Con International, in 2013, 2015, 2016, and

again in 2017. At the 2015 con, John and his coauthors, Andrew Aydin and Nate Powell, walked with arms linked to re-create the stance he took during the Selma march for civil rights. Hundreds and hundreds of con attendees joined them. The Comic-Con march was so popular, John led it again in 2016 and 2017.

CHAPTER 8
The End of a Life of Good Trouble

On December 29, 2019, John made a very serious announcement. He told the world that he had pancreatic cancer. Even though he was ill and being treated for the cancer, John returned to Congress to work and fight his disease until the very end.

"I have been in some kind of fight—for freedom, equality, basic human rights—for nearly my entire life. I have never faced a fight quite like the one I have now," John said.

John recorded a virtual town hall with former president Barack Obama so people could ask questions and speak with John and President Obama. John also gave a speech at Black Lives Matter Plaza in Washington, DC, in June 2020.

On July 17, 2020, John died at the age of eighty in Atlanta after an eight-month battle with cancer. Friends, family, fans, and colleagues in Congress offered prayers to the man who had spent his life fighting for freedom and justice in America.

Flags were flown at half-staff to honor John. Sweden's prime minister Stefan Löfven, France's president Emmanuel Macron, Ireland's president Michael D. Higgins, and many other world leaders offered tributes to John.

Many ceremonies were held to honor John. They began in Troy, Alabama, at the very school that rejected John's college application in 1957. A memorial was held at the Brown Chapel AME Church in Selma, Alabama, the church where the march to Montgomery was planned.

Brown Chapel AME Church

A horse-drawn carriage took John's casket over the Edmund Pettus Bridge, following the same path John had taken as a young man on the Bloody Sunday march from Selma to Montgomery.

When the carriage arrived in Montgomery, it was placed in the Alabama State Capitol, where mourners could pay their last respects to a home state hero. John's supporters began to call for the Edmund Pettus Bridge to be renamed after John. John was the first Black lawmaker to lie in state in the United States Capitol rotunda. To lie in state means John's casket would sit in a place of honor where people who admired him could pass by to say a final goodbye.

His final funeral service was at Ebenezer Baptist Church in Atlanta. Former American presidents Barack Obama, George W. Bush, and Bill Clinton spoke at the funeral. Barack Obama delivered the eulogy, a speech that recalled the amazing life of John Lewis.

John was laid to rest at Atlanta's South-View Cemetery on July 30, 2020.

The last thing John wanted was for any of his hard work to be undone once he was gone. The John R. Lewis Voting Rights Advancement Act of 2021 restored the power of the original Voting Rights Act of 1965. It required states with histories of voter discrimination and suppression to get approval from the Department of Justice before enacting voting changes.

Even after his death, John was remembered in special ways. Troy University (formerly Troy State College) renamed the main building on its home campus after John. The building, the oldest on campus, was previously named for a former governor or Alabama, Bibb Graves— a high-ranking member of the Ku Klux Klan.

The Edmund Pettus Bridge, named for Confederate general and Ku Klux Klan leader Edmund Pettus, will be renamed the Edmund W.

Pettus-Foot Soldiers Bridge by legislation passed by the Alabama Senate in 2022. John was awarded a Congressional Gold Medal in 2016 for being one of the "foot soldiers" in the fight for civil rights. The bridge's new name honors John's early civil rights activism.

On what would have been his eighty-first birthday, John was remembered by President Joe Biden. The president called on all Americans to continue John's work. "While my dear friend may no longer be with us, his life and

President Joe Biden

legacy provide an eternal moral compass on which direction to march. May we carry on his mission in the fight for justice and equality for all."

The Ku Klux Klan

The Ku Klux Klan was founded in 1865 after the Civil War to persecute and suppress the rights of freed enslaved people and to promote white supremacy. The name comes from the Greek word *kuklos*, which means "circle." The word *Klan* was added to mirror "clan" or a group of families. Klan members wore white hoods and robes and carried out brutal and illegal acts of violence,

usually under the cover of darkness at night.

Though it is considered a domestic terrorist organization, the Ku Klux Klan is permitted to carry out marches and rallies and to publish their beliefs and make speeches under the protection of the First Amendment.

The organization's targets are African Americans, Jewish people, Latinos, Asian Americans, Native Americans, Muslims, Catholics, atheists, immigrants, liberals, and LGBTQIA+ people.

John, who always planned ahead, left final words of wisdom behind. He wrote an op-ed (an article that expresses the opinion of the author) titled "Now It's Your Turn," that was published in the *New York Times* on July 30, 2020, the day of his funeral. John's newspaper article was a call for younger people to continue working for justice and an end to hate.

"Ordinary people with extraordinary vision can redeem the soul of America by getting in what I call good trouble, necessary trouble," John wrote. "Voting and participating in the democratic process are key. The vote is the most powerful nonviolent change agent you have in a democratic society. You must use it because it is not guaranteed." John meant that voting is an important and powerful right, and that we have to protect it in order to keep it.

Timeline of John Lewis's Life

1940 — John Robert Lewis is born just outside of Troy, Alabama, on February 21

1961 — Graduates from American Baptist Theological Seminary with a bachelor's degree in religion

— Enrolls at Fisk University

1963 — Gives speech during the March on Washington for Jobs and Freedom

— Becomes head of SNCC

1965 — Beaten and hospitalized during the march from Selma to Montgomery, Alabama, to protest voter suppression of Black people

1968 — Marries Lillian Miles on December 21

1986 — Elected to the US House of Representatives, representing Georgia's Fifth District

2011 — Awarded the Medal of Freedom by President Obama

2016 — Wins the National Book Award for Young People's Literature for his graphic novel *March: Book Three*

— Leads sit-in on the floor of the House of Representatives to protest lack of gun reform

2019 — Becomes third longest-serving Black member of Congress

2020 — Visits Black Lives Matter Plaza in Washington, DC, in June

— Dies from pancreatic cancer on July 17

Timeline of the World

1940 — President Franklin D. Roosevelt becomes the first three term president of the United States

1958 — The United States successfully launches the Explorer 1 satellite into orbit three months after the Soviet Union (now Russia) sent its first satellite

1960 — Police kill sixty-nine people in the Sharpeville Massacre after Black South Africans protest laws restricting their movement among white people

1969 — American astronauts Neil Armstrong, Buzz Aldrin, and Michael Collins achieve the first moon landing

1975 — The movie *Jaws*, directed by Steven Spielberg, is released on June 20, becoming the first summer blockbuster

1980 — The XIII Winter Olympics are held at Lake Placid, New York

1991 — Sharon Pratt Dixon is sworn in as mayor of the District of Columbia, becoming the first African American woman to be mayor of a major American city

2000 — Sony releases the PlayStation 2 gaming console in Japan

2020 — Kim Ng is named general manager of the Miami Marlins, becoming the first woman and first East Asian American to hold the position in the history of Major League Baseball

Bibliography

*Books for young readers

*Armand, Glenda. *Black Leaders in the Civil Rights Movement: A Black History Book for Kids*. Emeryville, CA: Rockridge Press, 2021.

*Asim, Jabari. *Preaching to the Chickens: The Story of Young John Lewis*. New York: Nancy Paulsen Books, 2016.

Lewis, John, with Michael D'Orso. *Walking with the Wind: A Memoir of the Movement*. New York: Simon & Schuster, 1998.

Lewis, John, with Brenda Jones. *Across That Bridge: A Vision for Change and the Future of America*. New York: Hachette, 2012.

Lewis, John, with Kabir Sehgal. *Carry On: Reflections for a New Generation*. New York: Grand Central Publishing, 2021.

Washington, Robin, dir. *You Don't Have to Ride JIM CROW!* 1995, New Hampshire: New Hampshire Public Television.